THE NEW PLAY

presents

The Pride of Parnell Street

Sebastian Barry

Fishamble Theatre Company is funded by the Arts Council/
An Chomhairle Ealaón and Dublin City Council.
The international touring of this production during 2007 and 2008
to London, Paris, Wiesbaden and New Haven
is supported by Culture Ireland.

Fishamble

Staff

Artistic Director	Jim Culleton
General Manager	Orla Flanagan
Acting General Manager	Marketa Puzman
Literary Officer	Gavin Kostick

Board

Eoin Kennelly (Chair), Siobhan Maguire, Stuart McLaughlin,
Jo Mangan, Vincent O'Doherty, Andrew Parkes

Fishamble wishes to thank the following
Friends of Fishamble for their invaluable support:

Robert & Lillian Chambers, Helen Cunningham, Brian Friel, Marian Keyes,
Jo Mangan, Vincent O'Doherty, Andrew & Delyth Parkes, Michael O'Connor,
John McColgan & Moya Doherty, David & Veronica Rowe, Dearbhail Ann Shannon.

Thank you also to those who do not wish to be credited

For details on how to become a Friend of Fishamble
please see www.fishamble.com or contact info@fishamble.com

Fishamble also wishes to thank the following
for their support with *The Pride of Parnell Street*:

Gerry Barnes and all at Cork Opera House, Brid Dukes and all at the Civic,
Una Carmody and all at the Helix, Monica Spencer, Peter McNamara and all at the Belltable,
Fergal McGrath and all at the Town Hall, Sarah Jane Leydon and all at the Hawk's Well,
Martin Murphy and all at the Pavilion, Sheila Pratschke and all at Centre Culturel Irlandais,
Beate Kronsbein, Dr Manfred Beilharz, Markus Bothe and all at the Neue Stucke Aus Europa
Festival Wiesbaden, Cathy Edwards and all at the Festival of Arts & Ideas New Haven,
Eugene Downes, Christine Sisk and all at Culture Ireland, John O'Kane, David Parnell
and all at the Arts Council, Jack Gilligan and all at Dublin City Council Arts Office,
Loughlin Deegan and all at the Ulster Bank Dublin Theatre Festival, Nicolas Kent and all
at the Tricycle, Maureen Kennelly and all at the Mermaid Arts Centre, Catherine Walsh,
Bianca Moore, Kieran Clifford and all at Amnesty International, Elaine Martin, Val Sherlock, and
all those who have helped Fishamble with the production since this publication went to print.

The commissioning of *The Pride of Parnell Street* was supported
by the Arts Council's Commission Award scheme.

Fishamble Theatre Company Ltd.
Shamrock Chambers
1/2 Eustace Street
Dublin 2, Ireland
Tel: +353-1-670 4018
Fax: +353-1-670 4019
E-mail: info@fishamble.com
Website: www.fishamble.com

The Pride of Parnell Street

by Sebastian Barry

Cast

JANET	Mary Murray
JOE	Karl Shiels

Director	Jim Culleton
Set & Costume Designer	Sabine Dargent
Lighting Designer	Mark Galione
Sound Designer	Denis Clohessy
Producers	Orla Flanagan
	Marketa Puzman
Literary Officer	Gavin Kostick
Production Manager	Des Kenny
Stage Director	Eavan Murphy
Stage Manager	Aaron Dempsey
Set Construction	Paul Manning
Hair & Make-Up	Aishling O'Donoghue
Graphic Design	Gareth Jones
Photography	Pat Redmond

The play is set in September 1999

The production runs for 100 minutes with no interval

The Pride of Parnell Street was first produced by
Fishamble: The New Play Company.
The production opened on 5 September 2007 at the Tricycle Theatre,
London, and then transferred to the Tivoli Theatre, as part of the
Ulster Bank Dublin Theatre Festival, and to the Mermaid Arts Centre.

It was nominated for *The Irish Times* Irish Theatre Award for
Best New Play 2007. In 2008, it toured in Ireland and internationally,
to the Centre Culturel Irlandais (Paris), Neue Stucke Aus Europa Festival
(Wiesbaden) and The Festival of Arts & Ideas (New Haven).

Fishamble: The New Play Company

About Fishamble The Company was founded in 1988 and, since 1990, has been dedicated to the discovery, development and production of new work for the Irish stage. Formerly known as Pigsback, the Company was renamed Fishamble in 1997. The name is inspired by Dublin's Fishamble Street and in particular, its playhouse which, in 1784, became the first Irish theatre to pursue a policy of producing new Irish work. Fishamble: The New Play Company has produced many plays by first-time and established playwrights in Dublin and throughout Ireland.

Fishamble Firsts The *Fishamble Firsts* scheme focuses on producing first plays by new writers. This includes recent productions such as *Noah and the Tower Flower* by Sean McLoughlin (2007), *The Gist of It* by Rodney Lee (2006) which was staged in New York by Origin/Fishamble, and *Monged* by Gary Duggan (2005) which won the Stewart Parker Trust Award, toured to Liverpool and was also staged in New York by Origin/Fishamble.

International Touring Fishamble has brought its work to the US, England, Scotland, Canada, Czech Republic, Romania, France and Germany. During 2008, Fishamble is touring *The Pride of Parnell Street* by Sebastian Barry (which opened in London in 2007) to the Centre Culturel Irlandais (Paris), Neue Stucke Aus Europa (Wiesbaden) and Festival of Arts & Ideas (New Haven), as well as touring *Forgotten* by Pat Kinevane to the Centre Culturel Irlandais (Paris), Kostel Na Pradle (Prague), International Theatre Festival (Sibiu) and Aurora Nova (Edinburgh).

Awards The Company's work has won a number of awards including *The Irish Times* Irish Theatre Awards, BBC/Stewart Parker Trust Awards, Dublin City Council Awards and *In Dublin* Theatre Awards. It has also been nominated or shortlisted for *The Irish Times* Irish Theatre Awards, Entertainment & Media Awards, PQ07, *The Irish Times* Living Dublin Awards, ZeBBie Awards and Allianz Business to Arts Awards. Recent awards include *The Irish Times* Irish Theatre Awards for *Whereabouts* (2006 Special Judges' Award) and for *Noah and the Tower Flower* (2007 Best New Play Award) as well as nominations in 2007 for *Forgotten* and *The Pride of Parnell Street*.

Publications Fishamble frequently works with publishers, including New Island Books, Nick Hern Books, Faber & Faber and Methuen, in order to extend the life of plays beyond production. In recent years, Fishamble has published every play it premieres. For further details of publications, see www.fishamble.com.

Partnerships Fishamble often works in partnership with arts and non-arts organisations. Recent and current partners include development agencies, venues and festivals throughout Ireland, as well as the Festival of Arts & Ideas (New Haven), Centre Culturel Irlandais (Paris), Tricycle Theatre (London), Aurora Nova (Edinburgh), Prague Fringe Festival, Neue Stucke Aus Europa (Wiesbaden), Amnesty International, RTÉ lyric fm, British Council Ireland, International Theatre Festival of Sibiu (Romania), TNL Canada, Ireland Newfoundland Partnership, The Gaiety School of Acting, Business to Arts, Origin Theatre Company (New York), Accenture, Allianz, National Association of Youth Drama, Liverpool Irish Festival, The Irish Council for Bioethics and Temple Bar Cultural Trust.

Training & Development   Fishamble runs many developmental initiatives and training projects, such as play development workshops, dramaturgical support, discussions, seminars, special events, and readings of commissioned and unsolicited work. The Company runs a programme of ongoing playwriting courses which are open to the public. These courses often form links with other new play companies, including Paines Plough and Tinderbox.

This strand of work also includes a mentoring scheme for Youth Theatre directors run in partnership with the National Association of Youth Drama, internships run with institutions including NUI and IES, off-site playwriting courses for literary, arts and theatre festivals nationwide, corporate training initiatives delivered in partnership with Business to Arts, and the *Fishamble New Writing Award*, launched in 2007, awarded to the best new writing in the Dublin Fringe Festival.

Future productions   As well as touring nationally and internationally in 2008, Fishamble will present the premiere of *Rank* by emerging writer Robert Massey. New work currently in development includes plays by Sean McLoughlin, Elizabeth Moynihan, Gary Duggan, Abbie Spallen and Gavin Kostick.

'Fishamble is to be congratulated on bringing original material to the public. It is ploughing a risky furrow to produce fresh, innovative and modern Irish writing for the theatre.'

Mary McAleese, President of Ireland

'Jim Culleton's work with new playwrights at Fishamble has detonated a controlled explosion of fresh talent.'

Fintan O'Toole

'In order to keep vibrant, theatre requires constant transfusions of new plays. This life-providing role is fulfilled enthusiastically and with wonderful results by Fishamble. Without them, Irish theatre would be anaemic.'

Brian Friel

Previous Productions of New Plays

2008

Forgotten by Pat Kinevane

2007

The Pride of Parnell Street
by Sebastian Barry
Noah and the Tower Flower
by Sean McLoughlin*
Forgotten by Pat Kinevane
(revival)

2006

Monged by Gary Duggan (revival)
Whereabouts
a series of short, site-specific plays by
Shane Carr,* John Cronin,* John Grogan,*
Louise Lowe, Belinda McKeon,*
Colin Murphy,* Anna Newell,*
Jack Olohan,* Jody O'Neill,*
Tom Swift and Jacqueline Strawbridge*
Forgotten by Pat Kinevane
The Gist of It by Rodney Lee*

2005

Monged by Gary Duggan
She Was Wearing . . . by Sebastian Barry,
Maeve Binchy, Dermot Bolger,
Michael Collins, Stella Feehily,
Rosalind Haslett, Roisin Ingle,*
Marian Keyes* and Gavin Kostick

2004

Pilgrims in the Park by Jim O'Hanlon
Tadhg Stray Wandered In by Michael Collins

2003

Handel's Crossing by Joe O'Connor,
The Medusa by Gavin Kostick,
Chaste Diana by Michael West
and *Sweet Bitter* by Stella Feehily
(a season of radio plays)
Shorts by Dawn Bradfield*,
Aino Dubrawsky*, Simon O'Gorman*,
Ciara Considine*, Tina Reilly*, Mary Portser,
Colm Maher*, James Heaney*,
Tara Dairman*, Lorraine McArdle*,
Talaya Delaney*, Ger Gleeson*,
Stella Feehily* and Bryan Delaney*
The Buddhist of Castleknock
by Jim O'Hanlon (revival)

2002

Contact by Jeff Pitcher and Gavin Kostick
The Buddhist of Castleknock by Jim O'Hanlon*
Still by Rosalind Haslett*

2001

The Carnival King by Ian Kilroy*
Wired to the Moon by Maeve Binchy,
adapted by Jim Culleton

2000

Y2K Festival
Consenting Adults by Dermot Bolger,
Dreamframe by Deirdre Hines,
Moonlight and Music by Jennifer Johnston,
The Great Jubilee by Nicholas Kelly,*
Doom Raider by Gavin Kostick,
Tea Set by Gina Moxley

1999

The Plains of Enna by Pat Kinevane
True Believers by Joe O'Connor

1998

The Nun's Wood by Pat Kinevane*

1997

From Both Hips by Mark O'Rowe*

1996

The Flesh Addict by Gavin Kostick

1995

Sardines by Michael West
Red Roses and Petrol by Joe O'Connor*

1994

Jack Ketch's Gallows Jig by Gavin Kostick

1993

Buffalo Bill Has Gone To Alaska by Colin Teevan
The Ash Fire by Gavin Kostick (revival)

1992

The Ash Fire by Gavin Kostick*
The Tender Trap by Michael West

1991

Howling Moons/Silent Sons by Deirdre Hines*
This Love Thing by Marina Carr

1990

Don Juan by Michael West

Biographies

SEBASTIAN BARRY   Author

Sebastian Barry is a major, internationally-renowned playwright and novelist. His plays include *The Pentagonal Dream* (1986, Damar Theatre, Dublin), *Boss Grady's Boys* (1988), *Prayers of Sherkin* (1990, Peacock Theatre), *White Woman Street* (1992, Bush Theatre), *The Steward of Christendom* (1995), *Our Lady of Sligo* (1998, Royal Court, Out of Joint), *The Only True History of Lizzie Finn* (1995), *Hinterland* (2002), a translation of Lorca's *The House of Bernarda Alba* (2003, Abbey Theatre) and *Whistling Psyche* (2004, Almeida Theatre). His awards include the BBC/Stewart Parker Trust Award, the Christopher Ewart-Biggs Memorial Prize, the Ireland/America Literary Prize, the Critics' Circle Award for Best New Play, the Writers' Guild Award, the Lloyds Private Banking Playwright of the Year Award and the Peggy Ramsay Play Award, as well as nominations for the Olivier Award and Man Booker Prize. Sebastian has also published several works of poetry and fiction, including the novel *The Whereabouts of Eneas McNulty* (Picador 1998), and *Annie Dunne* (Faber and Faber 2002). His novel *A Long Long Way* (Faber and Faber) won the Kerry Group Fiction Award, was short listed for the Booker Prize 2005 and the International Impac Dublin Literary Award, and was the selected title of the 2007 *Dublin: One City, One Book* initiative of Dublin City Council. His new novel *The Secret Scripture* (Faber and Faber, and Viking in the USA) is published this year. It will be published in Germany by Steidl and in France by Gallimard.

MARY MURRAY   Janet

This is Mary's second time working with Fishamble having recently played Natalie in *Noah and the Tower Flower* (*The Irish Times* Irish Theatre Award for Best New Play 2007). Other theatre work includes *Splendour* with RAW Productions, *The Alice Trilogy* with the Abbey Theatre, for which she received the *Irish Times* 'Best Supporting Actress' Theatre Award, *Sleeping Beauty* for Landmark Productions, *Macbeth* with Second Age, *Operation Easter* and *Five Kinds Of Silence* with Calypso Productions, *Family Stories* for B*spoke Theatre Company, *Sister* with Visions Productions, *Oh When The Hoops* with Liberty Productions, *Playing Politics* as part of the Dublin Theatre Festival, *Knocknashee* with Tall Tales, *The Grapes Of Wrath* with Storytellers Theatre Company, *Give Us A Break* and *The Shadow Of A Gunman* both for Tobarnarun and *On Raftery's Hill* – a co-production with Druid and The Royal Court (which performed at the Eisenhower, Washington D.C., the Royal Court in London, Galway Town Hall and the Gate in Dublin). Her film and television credits include: *Little White Lies*, *El Juego Del Ahorcado*, *No Laughing Matter*, *Prosperity*, *Frankie Bitterness*, *What If?*, *IRA King Of Nothing*, *Adam And Paul*, *W.C.*, *The Magdalene Sisters*, *On The Edge*, *Accelerator*, *Crushproof*, *A Great Party*, *Recoil*, *The Marriage of Strongbow and Aoife*, *The Very Stuff*, *ER*, *Fair City*, *Love Is The Drug*, *The Big Bow Wow*, *Ambassador* and *Random Passage*. Mary has also worked with RTÉ Radio on *Lennon's Guitar* and *The Sorting Office Of The Universe*. Mary is a multi award winning singer and the director of Visions Drama School.

KARL SHIELS   Joe

Karl trained at the Gaiety School of Acting, Dublin. Theatre credits include: *Romeo and Juliet* (Abbey Theatre), *Sleeping Beauty* (Helix), *Oedipus Loves You* (international tour), *Howie the Rookie* (Peacock, Bush, international tour), *Duck* (Peacock, Royal Court, UK tour), *Beauty in a Broken Place*, *Henry IV*, *Barbaric Comedies*, *Twenty Grand*, *At-Swim-Two-Birds* (Abbey, Peacock), *Salome* (Gate), *The Shadow of a Gunman* (Lyric), *The Duchess of*

Malfi, Early Morning, The Massacre @ Paris, This Lime Tree Bower, Quartet, Muller's Medea, Hamlet, The Spanish Tragedy, Greek (Project Arts Centre), *Comedians* (Best Actor at the 1999 Dublin Theatre Festival). Film and television credits include: *Get Rich or Die Trying, Eden, Batman Begins, Prosperity, Waiting for Dublin, Intermission, Veronica Guerin, Mystics, Spin the Bottle, Virtues of a Sinner, The Anarchic Hand Affair, Meeting Ché Guevara and the Man from Maybury Hill, Freaky Deeky 10/11, Clubbing, Daybreak, Capital Letters* (nominated for Best Actor, 2004 Irish Film and Television Awards), *Doctors, Attachments* (BBC), *Any Time Now, Camera Café, The Clinic, On Home Ground, Private Lives* (RTE). Karl is Artistic Director of Semper Fi (Ireland). Directing credits include: *Butterflies, Conversations with a Cupboard Man, Ten, Slaughter, Breakfast with Versace, Within 24 Hours, Another 24 Hours, Within 24 Hours of Dance, The Pitchfork Disney, Adrenalin,* and the multi award-winning *Ladies and Gents* (Semper Fi), *Eggshell, Drapes* and *Bernard Opens Up* (Fishamble), *Topdog Underdog* and *Three Tall Women* (Tall Tales).

JIM CULLETON   Director

Jim Culleton is the Artistic Director of Fishamble for which he most recently directed *Noah and the Tower Flower* by Sean McLoughlin (*The Irish Times* Theatre Award for Best New Play), *Forgotten* by Pat Kinevane (throughout Ireland and to Paris, Prague and Edinburgh), short plays for *Whereabouts* (*The Irish Times* Theatre Special Judges' Award) and *Monged* by Gary Duggan (Stewart Parker Trust Award winner) in Liverpool and as a staged reading in New York. He has also directed for Amnesty International, Pigsback, 7:84 (Scotland), Project Arts Centre, Amharclann de hIde, Tinderbox, The Passion Machine, The Ark, Second Age, RTE Radio 1, the Belgrade, The Abbey/Peacock, Semper Fi, TNL Canada, Scotland's Ensemble @ Dundee Rep, Draíocht, Barnstorm, TCD School of Drama, Origin (New York) and RTE lyric fm. His productions have won or been nominated for numerous awards, including *Irish Times* Theatre Awards, Entertainment & Media Awards, In Dublin Theatre Awards and TMA Awards. He co-edited *Contemporary Irish Monologues* and edited *Fishamble/Pigsback: First Plays* both for New Island Books and has edited/contributed to books for Carysfort Press, Ubu and Amnesty International. He most recently directed a special edition of *The Business* for RTE Radio 1, a reading of *My Name is Rachel Corrie* for Amnesty International and a production of *Monged* for the Belgrade.

SABINE DARGENT   Set & Costume Designer

Sabine is a French designer living in Ireland. Her work with Jim Culleton and Fishamble includes *Monged* by Gary Duggan (also at the Belgrade), *Pilgrims in the Park* by Jim O'Hanlon and *Tadhg Stray Wandered In* by Michael Collins. Recent works include, with Conall Morrison, *Scenes From The Big Picture* (Waterfront, Belfast), *The Bacchae of Baghdad* (Abbey Theatre), *The Importance of Being Earnest* (Abbey Theatre), *Antigone, Hard to Believe* (Storytellers Theatre Company) and *Ghosts* (Lyric Theatre, Belfast) for which she won the ESB/*Irish Times* Best Set Design Award in 2003 and, with Mikel Murfi, *The Lonesome West* (Lyric) and *The Walworth Farce* (Dublin, Edinburgh Fringe best yahoo written by Enda Walsh, Druid Theatre; *Irish Times* Award 2006, with her set design *Hysteria* for B*spoke), with Paula McFettridge, *Henry and Harriet* (Belfast) and *To have and to hold* (Old Museum Belfast), with Raymond Keane, *Circus* (nominated for best set design with *To have and to hold*, see above), with Roy Headberd, *Days of wine and roses* (Lyric), with Pat Talbot, *Dublin Carol* (Everyman Palace). Sabine also designed *How many miles to Babylon?* by Jennifer Johnston (Second Age, David Parnell), *The Shadow of the Glen, The Tinker's Wedding* (Big Telly), *Martha* and *Little Rudolf* (Barnstorm), *Jack Fell Down, Burning Dreams* and *Last Call* (Team), *The Tempest* (Blue Raincoat), *Desert Lullaby* by

Jennifer Johnston (Galloglass). She designed and performed painting in *Senses* (Rex Levitates). In France she designed for TGV and was in-house design assistant to Serge Noyelle (Theatre de Chatillon) and Antonio Diaz Florian (l'Epee de Bois). She was an assistant to Lucio Fanti on *En attendant Godot* by Beckett directed by Bernard Sobel (Theatre de Gennevilliers). Sabine has been working mostly in theatre, but also on film and exhibition, and she is currently designing a part of the St Patrick's Festival named City Fusion.

MARK GALIONE   Lighting Designer

In Ireland, Mark's lighting designs include work for The Peacock, The Civic, Classic Stage Ireland, Fishamble, Barabbas, Guna Nua, Cois Ceim, Hands Turn, Mask, Vesuvius, Dance Theatre of Ireland, Irish Modern Dance Theatre, High Resolution Lighting, Production Services Ireland, The Waterfront, The Ark and Calipo. In Britain, he has designed for Nigel Charnock, Gaby Agis, Sadler's Wells, The Royal Ballet, Ricochet, Small Axe, Soho Theatre Co, The Sherman Theatre and Emilyn Claid. For Fishamble, Mark has lit *The Y2K Festival, Still, Shorts, Tadhg Stray Wandered In, Pilgrims In The Park, Monged* and *Noah and the Tower Flower.*

DENIS CLOHESSY   Sound Designer

Denis's work includes *Fool for Love, Romeo and Juliet, Woman and Scarecrow, The Crucible* and *Julius Caesar* for the Abbey Theatre. *Macbeth, Titus Andronicus, Shutter, La Musica, Fando and Lis* (Siren Productions), *The Pride of Parnell Street* (Fishamble), *Is This About Sex?, Attempts on Her Life, Don Carlos, Dream of Autumn* (Rough Magic), *Festen* (Gate Theatre), *Alice in Wonderland, Sleeping Beauty, Underneath the Lintel* (Landmark), *Rashomon, The Dream of a Summer Day, The Crock of Gold, Mushroom* (Storytellers) , *Bones, Talking to Terrorists, Operation Easter* (Calypso) *Hysteria, Family Stories, Tejas Verdes* (b*spoke), *Last Call, Devotion, How High is Up* (TEAM), *Splendour, Winter, The System* (RAW), *Behindtheeyeliesbone* (Myriad Dance), *King Ubu* (Fineswine/Galway Arts Festival), *Same Same but Different* and *A Splendid Mess* (Locus). He has just completed the score for the documentary feature film *A Bloody Canvas* for Fastnet films. Denis has also composed for a number of short films including the European Academy Award winning *Undressing My Mother* and *Useless Dog* (Venom Films), for which he won Best Soundtrack at the 2005 European Short Film Biennale. Denis is an associate artist of the Abbey Theatre.

ORLA FLANAGAN   Producer

Orla is General Manager of Fishamble and has previously produced the Company's productions of *Noah and the Tower Flower* by Sean McLoughlin (*The Irish Times* Theatre Award Winner for Best New Play, 2007), *The Gist of It* by Rodney Lee, *Forgotten* by Pat Kinevane, a revival tour of *Monged* by Gary Duggan and the site-specific, multi-writer production of *Whereabouts* (*The Irish Times* Theatre Award winner 2006). Prior to this, she was the Literary Officer at the Abbey Theatre since 2001. She has also worked as Marketing Administrator at the National Concert Hall and has produced a number of shows for the Dublin Fringe Festival. In 2005, she worked as a trainee dramaturg at the Sundance Theatre Lab, Utah, and the Schaubuhne's Festival of International New Drama 05, Berlin. Orla is currently participating in an arts management fellowship programme at the John F. Kennedy Centre for the Performing Arts in Washington D.C., for which she has been awarded the Diageo Sponsored Fulbright Award for the Performing and Visual Arts.

MARKETA PUZMAN   Producer

Marketa has ten years experience of working in film and TV, both in the Art and Production Departments, in the Czech Republic. During her time in the film business, Marketa worked on 17 feature films - credits include *Hart's War*, *Les Misérables*, *Last Holiday*, *Van Helsing* and many television projects including BBC's *The Scarlet Pimpernel* series. Since relocating from Prague to Dublin, Marketa has worked in performing arts management, initially in contemporary dance as General Manager with Dance Theatre of Ireland, until she recently joined Fishamble, for which she produced *The Pride of Parnell Street*, revival tour of *Forgotten* and a reading of *My Name Is Rachel Corrie* in association with Amnesty International.

GAVIN KOSTICK   Literary Officer

Gavin is the Literary Officer for Fishamble. He works with new writers for theatre through script development, readings and a variety of courses. Gavin is also an award-winning playwright. He has written over a dozen plays which have been produced in Dublin, on tour around Ireland, the UK, New York, Philadelphia and Romania. His most recent works are *Olive Skin Blood Mouth* for the Gaiety School of Acting at Project Arts Centre and *An Image for the Rose* outdoors for Whiplash Theatre Company. He is currently working on new plays for Fishamble and Whiplash, and an Opera with composer Raymond Deane for RTE Lyric. For Dublin Fringe Festival 2007 he performed Joseph Conrad's *Heart of Darkness* complete, the production winning the Spirit of the Fringe award.

AISHLING O'DONOGHUE   Make-Up

Aishling trained in Media Makeup in the Somerset College of Art and Technology. Since her return to Ireland in 2002 she has worked in theatre with the Gaiety School of Acting (*Universal Export-Day Shift*, A.S.L.), Troubadors (*A Communication Cord*, *Loot*), Biscuits for Breakfast (*Naked Will*), Fishamble (*The Pride of Parnell Street*) and PurpleHeart Theatre Company (*Bug*). Aishling has also worked on many short films including *Nun* directed by Vittoria Collona which was shown at the Venice Film festival.

DES KENNY   Production Manager

Credits include *Noah and the Tower Flower*, *Pilgrims in the Park*, *Tadhg Stray Wandered In*, *The Gist Of It* and *Monged* for Fishamble, *Far Away*, *Urban Ghosts* and *Shooting Gallery* for Bedrock, *Alone It Stands* for Lane Productions and Yew Tree Theatre Company, *Triple Espresso* for Lane Productions, *Dublin by Lamplight*, *Mud* and *Everyday* for The Corn Exchange, *Sleeping Beauty* for Landmark/Helix and *How Many Miles to Babylon*, *Macbeth* and *Othello* for Second Age.

EAVAN MURPHY   Stage Director

After completing a course in Art and Design, Eavan studied Theatre Production at Colaiste Stiofan Naofa in Cork. She now works in many varied productions, including *La Traviata* (Opera Ireland); *Improbable Frequency* (including Edinburgh Festival and Kontakt Festival in Poland) and *The Bonefire* (Rough Magic Theatre Company); *The Barber of Seville* (Opera Theatre Company); three Irish tours of *I, Keano* (Lane Productions); *Madame T* (Meridian Theatre Company); *Hansel and Gretel* (Cork Opera House); *The Train Show* (Cork Midsummer Festival); *The Little Mermaid* (Big Telly Productions); *The Nutcracker* (The Point Theatre); *The Podge and Rodge Show* (Vicar Street, Double Z Productions). Eavan is delighted to have been invited back to work with Fishamble again, after stage directing the première of *The Pride of Parnell Street* in September.

Sebastian Barry
The Pride of Parnell Street

faber and faber

First published in 2007
by Faber and Faber Limited
Bloomsbury House, 74-77 Great Russell Street,
London WC1B 3DA

This revised reprint 2008

Typeset by Country Setting, Kingsdown, Kent CT14 8ES
Printed in England by CPI Bookmarque, Croydon, CR0 4TD

A CIP record for this book
is available from the British Library

978-0-571-24366-2

2 4 6 8 10 9 7 5 3

For Catriona Crowe

Characters

Janet
Joe

THE PRIDE OF PARNELL STREET

September 1999. Janet is a Dublin woman of about thirty-three years of age. She wears the day clothes of a normal inner-city person: jeans and maybe a hooded jacket. She sits on a nondescript chair downstage left.

In the shadows to the right, lies her husband, Joe, on a bed – might be a hospital bed. He's a good-looking man, some years older than Janet, but with his close-cut hair he looks rough enough. He has a thin gold chain around his neck. He's very thin.

Their accent is the Dublin accent of the area around Parnell Street, north of the Liffey.

There might be a suggestion in the stage design of a number of things, the old ESB power station in Ringsend, maybe the old water conduit that used to pour out of it that Joe wanted to clean himself in, or other places of the play.

There can be bits of music, Thin Lizzy and other bands and songs mentioned in the play, where needed – maybe inside speeches, and certainly between, wherever is thought useful. The actors might stay where they are, or move about, as instincts dictate. Even Joe might want to get out of bed for certain very active speeches, and get back in again and resume his illness. The lighting should be helpful to the actors, and not necessarily naturalistic. There might be certain effects, of Dublin sunlight and so on, not necessarily where they are mentioned, but echoing things said, as comfort, or warning. It is not a naturalistic space, except in the last scene perhaps. It is all the places they have been and know, and describe, just as they embody all their ages and deeds. Whether they are aware of each other before the last scene is up to the actors' instincts.

Light up clearly on Janet, who at last raises her eyes and looks straight out, with her fearless nature evident. She fingers the gold band of her wedding ring.

Janet In them days – in them days, long long ago, it seems like, when we was girls only really ourselves – sounds like some storybook, but. Me, I'd had the three boys already, Billy, Jack and little Macker. I was sixteen years old when I had Billy. Then the other two, on the trot, really. Yeh, and I was hoping for a little girl, you know, the way you do, but we thought we'd better call a truce at three, me and their da. Big Macker was their da, me husband, but I called him Joe, because that was his real name. It was his ould mother called him Macker, you know?

He was what was called a Midday Man. A Midday Man did get up at midday and he goes along the cars and looks for open cars and then he goes in and takes what he can find. And then down to Parnell Street to the Afternoon Man, he was a man that sat in the '98 pub, and he took in the stuff and gave cash on it, in the jacks like. And I was often told to go and do the same when the husband was laid up with flu or the like, and then I was a Midday Woman – you might say. But – that was how it was, in them days.

In them days – I'm fucking counting on me fingers and it's only nine years ago and it could be ninety, for all the changes. And here comes the new fucking millennium, just around the corner, and I suppose we're like the scrawny little kid on the seesaw, balancing in the middle, while his two mates bang the seesaw up and down at either end, in the ould playground on Hill Street as may be.

In them days was before the Africans came to Parnell Street and it was only ourselves knocking around and drinking in the pubs there. The kids played on the pavements outside the pub while we drank so we knew where they were. My Billy catched on the back of a beer lorry the O'Connell Street end of Parnell Street, and was dragged in the back of it somehow, how it happened only God knows, and when the driver heard people screaming at him, screaming at him they were, he stopped and got out of his cab, and found poor Billy all bundled up somehow in the what-ja-me-call-it, the fender round the back wheels. We didn't have no money that time as usual and we had to bury little Billy in the Angels' Acre, the plot of ground in Glasnevin where stillborn babbies and small childer was put. When they died. We stuck up a bit a' wood for a cross with 'Billy' wrote on it and his ma put a dome of plastic flowers where she thought the little chest might be.

He was only six.

It was an awful pity we didn't have the money for a headstone, you know.

Then when we had done our crying over that, Joe caught the middle child Jack at the same lark and he ran after and didn't he give him a right thrashing for that, because he was still as sad as Marlon Brando after what happened to Billy.

So maybe Joe was like a fella gets a taste of blood, hitting something smaller than himself, you know?

And not that it done Jack any good. He was always a holy terror. Him and his mates used to go up North Great George's Street, trying all the car locks as they went. They used to practise on the older cars, ould Fords from the seventies, because you could open them with a screwdriver. In them days that street was bumper to bumper with cars, and if Jack and his mates wasn't educating themselves on the locks, they liked to go up the whole street on the backs of the cars, never touching the pavement once. If they came to a car they knew, you know, if they knew the owner, someone that lived on the street as may be, they might go around that car, in a friendly way. I mean, Sinéad O'Connor lived on the street that time, and to Jack and his mates that ould beamer she drove was like a holy fucking relic. They'd never a' walked over that. Never. Your man from The Pogues lived there too, but, he didn't drive a car, for obvious reasons. I mean, you never saw him without a beer in his paw.

Of course, Joe couldn't say much to Jack about all that, considering his own line of work. But.

Jesus, it was like fucking Hollywood, North Great George's Street, that time, but without the palm trees.

We were all rubbing along together, I suppose.

Well.

Now Joe was always good enough in his way, his mother was from North Summer Street, his father had a scrapyard in the garden at the back instead of flowers, you know – Joe used to be sent as a little lad out to Ringsend on his own to bring back pram wheels, I don't know why there were so many prams dumped out by the power station, but there were. And he used to go swimming at the Shelly Banks in the summer in his knicks, while he was on the job like, and he always did say that was the happiest days of his life.

It wasn't a real job, was it?

He wanted to get a job at the power station because he knew the workers there washed the coal off themselves in this river of hot water that came out of the power station, it was after cooling the engines, and they had soap stuck in the walls of the river, and Joe liked all that, he said it was a grand life. But he never had a job in his life, other than being a Midday Man like I said.

In them days the Irish were doing real well at the football and after getting over the surprise of that, we began to think we could win the World Cup maybe and that lifted the spirits. That was a queer thing. 1990 it must have been, right? After a victory the whole of O'Connell Street would be like a bleeding party, and lads going crazy, and girls, and fellas falling down drunk and pissing on the statues, and general happy mayhem.

So now here we come to the hard bit of me story – you know, like a hard sum at school. I suppose there'd be a couple of hard bits actually.

To be winning the matches was a great ould thing and a great ould feeling was caused in us, me too included, and me boys were delighted and the whole flats was delighted and we'd go into Lucky Duffy's and she was delighted – she was a great woman, the queen of Parnell Street – and the filth would be looking happy too, though they was mostly country fellas and GAA men really, but.

And that was all great.

And it was summertime, you know, and Dublin in the summertime is just lovely, with the leaves on the old trees and the baking tar smells and just the way the breeze smelling of the sea goes along the old streets – but you know all that – sure why would we live in Dublin iffen we didn't adore her?

But I was saying – the first match we won Joe comes home in the small hours, he was right tanked, and that was all right, but he had pissed down his trousers and he was all in a twist sort of about something but not having the words to say what. He musta bought a soccer jersey in the street, it was size small, and he gives it to me, beaming he was.

He was happy, high happy, like a crazy happy, a big blank happy look on his musher like he was on some bad drug, but he never done that. And that was very queer, and me and the little lads kinda slunk off in a corner and let him – blow up like a balloon – roaring and happy as a king – kinda bursting he was – then in the morning, like a balloon left sitting for a week he was, the sag in his face and the low throttle in his poor voice. Oh, yes.

And we was winning and winning. You remember?

But did we ever score a goal?

I don't think so.

It was always a draw, or some kinda advantage, or some kinda squirming through by a miracle – but no, we musta scored a goal, we musta scored *one*.

There was nothing but happiness them days for Joe. You'd swear he was after playing in the games himself, 'we' done this and 'we' done that, and 'the lads' were after doing such and such, and saying such and such – and maybe that was the trouble.

Now thinking about it all these years later, because Janey it must be near ten year ago, before even the Africans came to Parnell Street, and got everyone wearing beads in their hair, and got old shops all new again – thinking about it, maybe that was the trouble. Maybe that was the trouble, the great yawning gap between – the fact that in the upshot, he wasn't a 'we', he wasn't winning nothing, he wasn't really *connected*, he was just fucking Joe, Joe Brady whose mother was from North Summer Street, and he was still getting up at midday and scouting the fucking cars, he was still a Midday Man, no matter what fucking countries we beat, and no nearer in all of eternity to washing himself in that wonderful river he was yearning for, yearning for, down at the Shelly Banks.

So this night he comes home, it was the night we got as far as the – was it the semi-final, or the quarter? I could not tell you at this distance – but we had got as far as we were going and although there was jubilation as the fella on the telly might say, yes, yes, there was something else also. There was something else like a crusher of stones, there was something else.

Joe came home from O'Connell Street. I was wearing the green jersey he had brung home for me the first time, I always wore it in bed on a match night, like instead of me T-shirt, to bring Joe luck. It was about four o'clock in the morning, and he was sober as a judge. I remember the lovely yellow light of the early morning sitting up in our bedroom window like some ould flower. He comes over to me half-asleep in the scratcher.

I was so glad to see him. I loved Joe, I knew everything about him, what he had to do to make a crust, and he was fond of his boys, he was, and he cried like a baby when Billy was killed, he cried for three days.

But what he was thinking of that time I do not know.

He comes over to the bed and I'm all warm like, you know the way you are, in the sheets in the summer, and sleepy, and glad to see him. 'How did it go, Joe?' I says, and he says, 'What did you say?' 'How did it go?' I says, and he looks at me all dark, and he comes over closer, and he sees the green jersey and he grabs it.

It was like a red rag to a bull, that green jersey, a red rag to a bull.

And he pulls me from the bed. It was all so sudden like. I couldn't believe it. I never had nothing from him before that but kindness, he depended on me, you know? For everything. I'd known him since I was four and he was a big fella of ten going round the place. And why it didn't stop him beating the shite out of me, I'll never know, as God is my witness.

I can't tell you all that he did – you wouldn't believe me. Joe!

And when I got away from him and grabbed Jack and Little Macker from the other room, and hurried down the stairs as best I was able, I did, I looked back up and he was on the balcony, roaring and spitting fire like a demented demon, that's what he was like.

Ran down the clattery iron stairs, bent almost double, and pulling on the little hands of me sons, to get them to come on.

And I went down to the Women's Shelter and by now I was moving really really slow and feeling me injuries something bad, because, you know, you're in shock for a little while at first, and numb, and the blood was pouring outa me nose, or somewhere, all down me fucking jersey, and me trying not to show too much for the boys' sake, them whimpering and looking about, and me weeping weeping, trying not to, I couldn't believe it, and by God if I tell a word of a lie, half the street was down there.

I wasn't the only one.

Like wounded bleeding soldiers we were after a battle.

It must have been like a fever. When the Irish team lost, the lads suddenly knew what was what. When the Irish team were winning they could pretend they were winning, but when they lost, they knew they were losers too – had never been winners in the first place! It must have been like bubbles bursting in their heads, bullshit bubbles. They couldn't stand it. There was a lot of happiness in them days and a lot of ould bullshit. That was the problem.

And then there was a lot of sorrow.

I went back to me mam's house in Portobello and she said me and the kids could stay with her. She was living up there because me mam's brother-in-law's sister had had a fixed rental and she was after up and dying and she sorta left the rental to me ma so she went over there living. Me ma was sick of living in the Wild West as she called it and me da would do anything for me ma, even including leaving his favourite haunts. I got her to swear she wouldn't say a word about what happened to me to me da, because I knew he'd only go spare. He had this really soft side to him, but when he was roused you couldn't stop him, because he was a fucking giant. I don't know what she told him, what with me bruises and whatnot, but as far as I know he never went after Joe. I was so glad because I didn't want me da up for murder. But he musta known really, because he was so nice to me and the boys, buying them ice creams every day and that sort a' thing, and he used to bring me flowers he'd pick along the Grand Canal on his way home.

Me poor da.

Anyway. I swore I would never go near Joe again.

It broke Joe's heart, a mate a' his told me a good while after, in the street. That was this awful skanky skanger called Jazzman Jack who never cared for nothing but drugs so maybe you couldn't believe him anyway.

I burned the green jersey in the mam's stove. It was like the fucking Turin Shroud with all the blood. Red rag is right. I didn't want to be seeing that again.

Since them days the Irish team has never done so good.
They got an eejit in after Jack Charlton to be looking
after things.

Thank God, I say.

But my heart has never mended neither. I've been going
about with a broken heart, the whole time. That's how it
is. I can't tell you any different.

*Light away from Janet mostly, although there's a little
left her, like stray light from a weak bulb.*

*Joe's light doesn't much improve, but there's stage light
given to his face, arms and hands. He has tattoos all
over himself and his skin is blotchy.*

Joe That time I was in prison, God be with the days,
I used to say to myself, When I get outa this place I'm
going to show the world what's what.

I used to say, I'm going to show the world what Joe Brady
can do.

When they have you in there, in the Joy, for a good
stretch like I been, you get to think an awful lot. Yes, sir.
For the first while you're just the same as you ever were,
thinking the world had it in for you, and was out to get
you, just you in particular. Set up that way, you know, by
whoever, God, or whatever.

The fucking inner city they call it, like it was something
inside something, something hidden inside, or safe inside,
I don't fucking know. But the place where I come from
is all raw in the wind, *outside* with fucking knobs on,
nothing fucking inner about it, it's as out as you can get,
like the North Pole.

And your emotions, you know, like the counsellors say
in there, your emotions are just the thoughts and suchlike

of the fella that's always outside, freezing, like an animal yourself, one of them polar bears like you'd see anytime in the zoo. You know in your heart of hearts that what the big fellas, I mean, the politicians, really want to do, is get rid of you, just clean all the shite out of Dublin, like the shite in the Liffey, and have a nice clean fucking perfect Dublin, so clean and so perfect the fucking salmon will climb up the river walls and walk about, happy as Larry.

So for the first bit that's how you're thinking. For the first year even maybe. And then you're thinking, how did I get into this fucking nightmare?

And that's when you really would want strong drugs.

Because a whole heap of stuff comes down on your head, like when you break into a ceiling in an old house, and all this ould shite and dust comes down on your head from the attics, you know, if you're doing demolition work on the buildings. Not that I ever done a gear job like that.

And that's if you're lucky. Because if that stuff never strikes you, you just go on the way you were, being a stupid bollocks, and using, and all the rest.

And I do wonder sometimes what being alive is for, I mean they call it the gift of life, and when I'm looking at some of me mates, I'm wondering what sort of fucking gift it is. I mean, God gives you the gift of life, and there might be a fella sitting in a cell there in Mountjoy, quietly getting the gear into himself, and his head locking back, and he's calming down, and feeling kinda okay again, and then he's at it again a few hours later, the poor bollocks, I mean, that's it, the whole thing for some of them lads, and I don't blame them, but, how can you call that the gift of life?

So these are some of the thoughts that begin to strike you, like, after that first little while when nothing strikes you.

And then the guilt comes down with all the rest, that's the third fucking phase, the fucking lousy feeling that it was all your own doing, it was you got yourself into this lousy fucking hole, and no one else.

And then in my case I'm thinking of her, I'm thinking of the most beautiful girl in the whole world, the fucking star of my life, you know, I'm thinking of Janet. And what I done. What I done to her, roaring and shouting and scaring her, and what I done after what I done to her.

And then I'm fucking raking and tearing at myself, at me own heart, I tell you, no one could really tell you what that feels like, unless you're after feeling it for yourself.

No one.

Janet, she was like someone in the films, someone you'd see at the pictures in O'Connell Street.

I'd be sitting beside her at the pictures as a matter of fact in the old days looking up at the screen at some young one in Hollywood, and thinking, I've someone just as fucking lovely sitting right beside me. Why wouldn't I think that?

When we was making love and she'd sit on top of me like, her breasts would sort of fall longer than they seemed most times, they got slimmer and pointier, pointing at me you know. Choosing me, it looked like. Electing me, like in an election.

And that used to make me crazy, crazy.

And then she'd be dressing in the morning and pulling on her jeans, over her lovely backside, and then some gear top I'd nicked for her in Arnott's on top of that, and

I swear to the good God, to the good Jesus, there was not another like her. I never seen no one like her anyhow. I was always glad I went and married her, I was always astonished she had agreed to marry me.

(*His wedding ring.*) I mean, a woman like that.

When she was a girl going about, you knew she never was going to end up like some of the others, you sort of knew.

Her mother was lovely-looking too, I think her whole family musta been like a family of film stars, they were that good-looking.

Except the da, he looked like a boxer because he worked on the big ships, and they were always in fights, the dockers, drinking fifteen pints of Guinness in a few hours between jobs and thinking nothing of it, and getting into big brawls with Norwegian sailors and great fucking giants of Nigerians and whatnot, just for the sport. They'd knock the bejaysus out of each other and then the next thing, they'd be in one of the pubs there singing sentimental songs together, with the blood and bruises all over them.

Drinking together like nothing happened.

I like that.

But they were like fucking kings, and Janet's da was one of them.

And I don't know and if he ever laid a finger on his missus, maybe he didn't, now I think of it. Because Janet would never have forgave that. Not that I ever hit Janet, no, I never did.

God is my witness.

No, I did not.

It was the Afternoon Man killed Janet's da. Stabbed him over a bet, or something, no one knew what.

He draws out a knife and stabs Janet's da through the chest.

There was this other fella there, a little skinny cunt from Cumberland Street, and he says:

'Stab him again, Dickie.'

Dickie was the Afternoon Man's name.

So he did.

That's how those things happen.

It was, like, done in a jiffy.

I hope you don't mind me telling you about Janet, her breasts and all.

I don't like to call them tits, like lads might.

They weren't tits, they were breasts. She had this face on her like a statue in the National Museum, if you were ever in there on a rainy afternoon, all smooth, and she had lovely black hair like a horse's tail.

I say had, but I am sure she has it still, only I haven't seen her this long while, what with me being in here in the ould hospital and her not wanting anything to do with me, much less come and visit her husband.

Because I am her husband still and I am very fucking proud of that, but all the same I don't think she thinks so any more.

Billy, you know, he'd be sixteen now if he had lived, and Jack and Macker can't be far behind.

Billy was the firstborn, he used ta give me goosebumps when I seen him, in his cot, that time he was born in the

Coombe. I used ta kiss him, you know, on his little nose, real proud I was. Well, he was mine, wasn't he? I helped Janet get him feeding at the breasts in the first days, would you believe, she was having awful trouble with it, and she was weeping she was. 'I'm no fucking good at this, Joe,' she says, and I said to her, 'It's the most natural thing in the world, the cows do it, the birds do it, it'll be no bother to you, Janet,' I said. 'The birds don't do it, Joe,' she said, but she was laughing, that little laugh she had, heh heh heh, and I don't know, maybe the little taps inside her got a shake or something, but the milk suddenly came. Oh, Jesus.

Billy was killed of course.

Jack and little Macker, me own sons. Makes me arms ache to think of them.

You can't help wondering what your sons look like, especially if you never do see them.

I wrote the hundred times in the Joy and said a hundred times I loved her and I was sorry, sorry for what I done, acting like a bowsie that fucking time Ireland lost, but you know, a hundred letters can't wipe out a sin, no, and I know that.

I know it only too well because I wrote the letters and she didn't come.

But also even the worst sin can't wipe out a love, you know?

But I was saying.

Jumping around a bit in me story.

Sorry about that.

I was talking about when I was to get out of prison, and the plan I had.

23

I'll be out next week, I was thinking, and they'll give me my bundle at the gate, and by Jesus I'm going to set the world to rights.

Because I knew I done everything myself, fucked it all up, and it was no one else's fault.

She's the loveliest woman in the world. You know the ould song, that the lad with the silver hair used sing, 'If you happen to see the most beautiful girl in the world, will you tell her – that I love her?'

All right, you're looking at me maybe and thinking this fucker's a dangerous-looking bastard. He's probably just a scaghead like the rest of them.

But I never done drugs, no, I did not.

Maybe you think if you sat up close to me, I'd be smelling, not even washed, you know, or give you some fucking disease, or I'd as soon knife you as look at you, like one of them geniuses down in the '98.

That I'm some bastard like that.

That done awful things, and deserved to be locked up in the Joy, and deserves to be here now, in the old *Bon Secours* hospital.

Is that German, or what?

Did you ever see *The Shootist* with John Wayne? Gear fucking film. Old cowboy dying, and John Wayne dying too, in real life.

What in the name of Jaysus is real life, when it's at home?

A bit of dark for Joe. Light again on Janet.

Janet Joe's ma, you know, she comes over to the house to speak to me. That's how I knew he was getting out. I wouldn't a' known any other way.

She was a real Northsider, she didn't like crossing the river, she didn't feel safe, she thought the Southsiders carried diseases like the rats, and her only coming from the worst street in Summerhill, North fucking Summer Street, where they boil and eat their young. Her own father was mucker-out for Sammy the Jew, the rag and bone man, who had his premises there on Parnell Street, and if that's not the filthiest job ever invented tell me what is. The smell from Sammy's would a' killed a horse, which wouldn't a' been the worst thing, since Sammy bought dead horses.

In them old days you could make a few bob from a dead horse, which just goes to show how useless we are in the present times.

You can only make money nowadays out a' good things.

Joe's ma was always talking against the Jews, even though there were none of them around any more, they were all gone on to Cleveland, Ohio, and living in mansions I am sure. It wasn't just the Jews she didn't care for, it was the Africans, and the Chinese, and the Romanians, and what have you. I heard her at it one day in the knicker department in Clery's, gassing away to an old crony of hers – 'They've tooken the best jobs off of the Irish and are only sponging off of the state.'

Her, whose son was a Midday Man and drawing the dole every week of his life.

So she crosses over O'Connell Bridge like a traveller crossing into a foreign territory. She was probably surprised there was no customs on the bridge, and that no one asked to see her passport.

She was a right determined little woman though. She was willing to risk the bit of foreign travel just for the pleasure of annoying the jaysus out of me.

The first thing in her way might have been my mam except she was out at her job cleaning the offices of that crowd along the canal that made cigarettes. Maybe they still do.

So I didn't have nothing between me and the knock on the door. So I just open it.

And there she is, already in a steam from the walk. The mush on her so tight you'd think she'd had a bleedin facelift. And I don't know if I wasn't a bit worried for her, because she had this awful high blood pressure and Joe was very fond of her.

But leaving that aside.

'Big Macker's getting out Monday,' she says.

'Oh,' I says, 'I have a barring order agin him and that's official,' I says.

She says, 'You must be the cruellest girl in Dublin.'

'Oh,' I says, 'I don't know, but, he won't be coming anywhere near us – and that's official.'

'You can say official as often as you like,' she says, 'but it don't make it right.'

'So what is right?' I says. 'Beating the living crap outa your wife?'

'He never done that,' she says. 'Everyone knows he is innocent, he never touched his wife.'

'Who are you talking to, Mrs Brady? Who's this standing in front of you? Hello? I am his fucking wife.'

'You are,' she says, 'and God help him. And I want me wheelier back,' she says.

'Your what?' I says.

'Me wheelier.'

'But sure that's like twelve years old,' I says.

She meant the fucking wheelier she bought for us when Billy was born, for the love of God.

'I fucking want it anyhow,' she says.

So I go to the ould cupboard where it was and I just gave it out to her.

And she turns about, with a very black look to her, and away she goes back down along the canal, with the ould wheelier, all stained with the puke and shite of yesteryear.

That would try the patience of a saint. And I'm no saint.

What do you reckon she was after? Me to take him back, me to feed him, wash his clothes? Maybe to save herself the bother, I don't know. Or maybe she was trying to do the right thing by her own son, I don't know. But if there's ever a vacancy in the diplomatic service I hope they don't fill it with her.

Anyways I was standing there again in the little living room and I was crying. Me two lads were at school, thank God.

Everyone cries, don't they? It's just natural.

Tension and that.

There's a good deal in life to make a woman cry, and that's just the way of it. Which is the why women are so nice to women in general, and get on, and like to have a drink together, and sing a few ould songs, like me da used to.

I was sorta thinking those thoughts.

Me da.

Me poor dead da, yeh.

Oh, torrents of tears then.

Yeh.

The fucking waterfall in Powerscourt if you was ever there. That me kingly da was killed by a scumbag like the Afternoon Man. Oh, Jesus. And my little fella killed along the same street. Two of the things closest to my heart. Gone. You can imagine the state of me then, in me mam's little sitting room.

His little fairy, he called me, now, which is a bit embarrassing. But he meant well. And every little girl looks like a little fairy, doesn't she? I always wished I had got a little girl, like I said. To be dressing her and that. But I got a lot a happiness too out a' the boys, yeh?

Billy died but the other two are just as nice.

They're old-fashioned Dublin boys in that they're nice to their ma. I don't know why, but they are. And I'm very glad a' that. I am. I wouldn't trade it for nothing. If you said to me, Janet, you can have a big house by the sea and all the tea in China, if you will give up your two sons, I would say – but you know what I'd say.

Anyone would.

Everyone loves their kids.

When I was a little girl and me da stood with the window behind him, he looked like there was gold all around his head. I remember actually even when I must a' been tiny, tiny, in one of them bouncy chairs you can get in Arnott's, must a' been, so was I even one year old? – I remember seeing him like that, like he wasn't even real. He used ta be singing 'Kevin Barry' and he never tired of that song and he used a be singing that, dawn to dusk, and when I was about three or four, he put me up on a table, and learned it to me, so I could be singing it to him.

(*Singing.*) 'Kevin Barry was a young lad, of the age of seventeen . . .'

And most important maybe above all, he never laid a hand on me ma like most men did in them days, and yeh, later days too. So when people do be criticising the world as an evil place with nothing to put in the balance of evil, like, I always think of me da, and me mam too, and the love that there was between them, before the bleeding Afternoon Man took it away for ever.

A pause for a bit.

See, love between a man and a woman, well . . . Joe done wrong, a' course he done wrong. He done the worst thing next on nigh killin' me. He killed me love, didn't he? I suppose he musta done. Next on nigh. And I didn't go back to him, like a lot a' girls do, no, I didn't. And I don't know why girls go back, but they do, every day of the week. But, when he was in his heyday, you know, when he was strong and really young and that, and Billy was just born, he was a good man to me. He wasn't like some of them young fellas, wouldn't be seen dead wheelin' a pram. Not that we had a pram. But we had the wheelier, you know, that nice wheelier that Joe's mam bought in the first flush, you know, when the little chiseller was born.

'My grandson.'

It was the Rolls-Royce of wheeliers, so it was.

And Joe would get up at six with Billy to let me sleep, and go off up to the Royal Canal Basin, just walking and singing. He loved Thin Lizzy because of Phil Lynott so he did, he saw the first concert Phil gave in the Abbey years before, Joe was there, Jaysus he couldn't a' been more than twelve, with his big sister maybe, he couldn't a' given a fuck about The Beatles in O'Connell Street, no, no, it was all Thin Lizzy, and he'd be singing 'The Boys

are Back in Town' to Billy when Billy was about two
months old, going up Blessington Street with the wheelier,
and the bottle and the nappies and all in a little bag for
themselves, should the need arise. And then there was the
little ballad Phil wrote for his own daughter that time.
Sara? (*Singing.*) 'My Sar-a . . .' Joe sung that too. In the
nice clear light of a Dublin morning. And me sleeping.
And the first steps that Billy took was along the Royal
Canal, and Joe said he just stepped around all the dog
turds like it was in his blood. A real Dubliner, you know?
And one time when Billy was sick, I can see it now in the
dark of the room, and Joe got up out a' the bed, I was so
tired I coulda slept through Hiroshima, and Joe hadn't a
stitch of clothes on him because it was summer then, and
he lifted out Billy and Billy, the little gangster, he pukes
into Joe's mush, talk about a waterfall, and it goes all
over him, from head to foot, and Joe standing there
laughing, and he cleans off Billy, and then he cleans off
himself, laughing the whole time, and sorta *pleased*, and
I thought to myself in the bed, Joe's a good father not be
getting annoyed, I mean . . . And I said it to him, and
I mighta said 'Joe, you just won the lottery,' Joe was that
chuffed. See, love between a man and a woman, it's –
private. It happens where you never do see it. In rooms.

   Light on Joe.

Joe So you're asking, what has me in here, the fucking
Bon Secours?

I got this awful fucking rash on me arm, this was a year
ago must have been, and then on me other arm, and then
all over me stomach and me chest. I looked like some
ould apple some ould one in Moore Street would be
trying to sell ya, putting it under a few shiny apples at the
top of the pile. Which is a talent. You know. Black bruises.
So I go to the Accident and Emergency and I swear to
Jesus, I see a young coloured doctor – after about two

hundred hours, you know – and when he sees me red and black marks, he steps back like I had the fucking plague. He has this big panicky look on his face. I sorta knew then I was in big fucking trouble.

'What's up, Doc?' I says, you know, the way you would.

'We'll have to take a blood-test,' he says, like he might a' said, might as well dig a hole for you straight away, his voice was that fucking weird.

So he gets a little nurse to put on the stretchy gloves and she takes some blood.

Looked all right to me. Red as it ever was.

Where they brung it I don't know, but I had a message about six weeks after, to be coming in to talk to them.

Well, fuck, I tell you, that was a bad day.

I was like a child all that day I don't mind telling ya.

I may a' been a bad bastard but I was very fond a' life.

Very.

Weeping, ya know?

But, leavin' that aside.

Where the fuck was I? Oh, yeh, me plan. I was just getting out a prison, wasn't I? Was that summer of '96? You'd think I'd know for sure, a thing like that. Where are we now? Is it fucking '99? Sometimes the ould head is just – swimming. But.

I do remember that the day I got outa prison I went straight to Burger King in O'Connell Street and ate a Whopper – with cheese. I had been promising meself that.

Then I went home to the ma like you do. She kept talking the whole time about me boys and how she wanted to see me boys, and that your woman, as she called Janet, had no right to keep them away from me, and I said, but ma, that's what she wants, that's what Janet wants, and anyway.

But of course I was missing the boys meself, Jack and little Macker, and I woulda given me eye teeth to see them. You want to be kissing your childer, you know? You can't help it. You do be dreaming of them, of their faces, and what they might be saying. So I was dying to see them. Because it was me life, me life before.

And to see Janet.

Just to see her. Look at her. After them years apart.

I knew she must look a bit older, you know. Not much, but a bit.

But I was older. A hundred years older.

Even then I looked like an ould fella in the little mirror in me ma's jacks. I was shooting inta me feet so the ma wouldn't know I was using, like Phil Lynott done. Mind you, I coulda been shooting inta me nose for all the ma knew, because she knew nothing about drugs. But it was a Thin Lizzy thing, you know.

Yeh, I know. I did say I never touched the scag. I did say that. I'm a fucking liar. I took me first hit with a good mate a' mine in this fucking awful hole of a kip in Cabra. It was only six months after Janet fucked off. He said it would cheer me up.

Now it did cheer me up, considerably.

So much so, by the end of that month, I was a fully paid-up member of the scag-artists' union.

You look alright for a while even on the gear. Then, not so fucking much. Then, not at all. Then not at all by any fucking means. It's a gradual thing.

I look a lot worse now, if that's possible. I have more holes in me body than a dead dog that the maggots have been eating. And I'm only thirty-fuckin'-nine as the crow flies, would ya believe? By Jesus.

Then me ma went over to try and talk to her. When I found out she had been and done that, I was ragin' with her. 'Ma,' I says, 'what in the name of Jaysus did you go and do that for? Jaysus, Ma,' I says.

Or was I still in the Joy when she went over? I can't remember. Because the ma came to see me every week, good as clockwork. She was always a very nice ma to me.

How and ever, you don't want your bollocking ma going doin' your work for you, do you? Anyhow, Jaysus, I knew it would take more than that to win her over. Something big was required. That's where me plan came in, me ould plan.

Something big, because there was yawning gaps in the things I ought to a' done for her. Fucking gaping chasms.

You'll be remembering I told you before about how her da died? Terrible tragic it was, and it done no one any good, and it happened about a year, year and a half, after Janet and me split up, so I never even could talk to her about it, and see how she was feeling.

She must a' been feeling shite.

And I would a' gone to the funeral and offered me condolences except the other thing happened before I could do that, and well, the Gardai had other plans for me then. When I think of how she must a' feeled, when that bastard went and put the knife in her da's chest.

And I wasn't able to comfort her. I wasn't in a position to, as you might say.

Janet had always been very nice to me. You could miss that the most, yeh, looking back, drinking the cups of tea together in the ould doss in the morning, just nattering about everything and nothing. A lot gets done, in the doss, like that. Decisions, and all that fucking lark. It's nice.

So –

'The other thing' – I've not said nothing about that either, have I?

It must a' been just before the time her father was killed. I was on the ould scag right enough even then, and as a matter of fact I was living rough up past the Morning Star hostel.

I wasn't in the hostel itself, there was a ould row of ould outhouses there with these mattresses in them and we scag-artists used to have our gear there and be living off the land like cowboys. You know.

We'd take a syringe full a' blood down to O'Connell Street and in a quiet moment when the Gardai were looking somewhere else, we'd show the syringe to a shopkeeper or a tourist and see what we could get.

It was much worse work than the Midday Man work but we were that little bit more desperate.

I didn't like to rob the tourists because, you know, Ireland of the Welcomes and all that, but, needs must in a tight situation.

And when we didn't make out in O'Connell Street, well, we went roving then up the river and into the Phoenix Park, to see what we could see.

There was a little river there in the park where this ould weed did grow, and the Chinese used to come there to gather the weed, whatever it was, to be putting in their soup for the takeaways I suppose. I mean, not all hours of the day, but it was them sort of people you could think to rob in the Phoenixer, innocent fellas not thinking of danger.

So I was up there roving one afternoon, or near enough to night, keeping an eye out for such class of people, roaming about through the bushes and the byways, one eye alighting here on a group of little queerboys cruising each other, and one eye there on the black water hens that did be making those hop, skip and jumps on the water, and the foul air going all red and dark what with the sun going down by Chapelizod – when I seen these two lads pitching a tent on the Fifteen Acres, where his Holiness John Paul II did alight in his helicopter.

Isn't 'alight' a very nice word? That's what happens in prison when you've nothing to do but to be reading books and dodging fellas trying to get a ride off your arse.

So his holiness alights from the helicopter and kisses the ground and then he says, 'Young people of Ireland, I love you.'

That was very nice of him.

Did you ever hear the like of that? But going back to that other business – them two lads.

Lads they were only, with rucksacks and a fucking tent, and a hammer and all for the pegs, and the bleeding chatter out of them, like they was in the wilds of Kerry.

I was with my mate from Cabra, Jazzman Jack they called him, because he loved what-ya-ma-call-him, Miles fucking Davis, yeh, he was always playing Miles Davis on his Walkman, and scag-artist like me though he was, I never did see him sell nor pawn that Walkman, he was that dedicated to his music.

So he goes up to these two young fellas and starts talking

to them very friendly like, and the young lads are laughing, and then Jack gives me a cold, hungry look like a wolf in a horror film, and he turns sudden nasty on them, and draws a blade, and he looks at them fair and square in the falling light, the two of them shivering like deer, and one of them gives me about two hundred nicker in notes like, and the other gives Jack his traveller's cheques, and Jack is fair fucking snarling at him, 'They're no fucking good, you got to sign them for me,' he says, and the lad, he was maybe German or French, didn't know what that was, and Jack grips his hand to show him what he meant, and the young lad leaps back, and then the other lad leaps forward, you know, one leaping back, one leaping forward, it would a' confused General Patton. 'You fucking German cunt,' says Jack, though he may have been French either, and in fact he was French, because it came up in court later. 'You fucking German cunt,' and he runs the knife into the German – the French lad I mean – but it doesn't go in, I mean it goes into the lad's wrist in some funny sort of way, and now the lad's leaping about with the knife caught somehow in his bleeding wrist, and screaming, and then Jazzman Jack shuts him up, I mean, shuts him up, and then this priest – I kid you not, what was he doing there in the park that time of night? – comes suddenly into view, and it's by no means easy to see a priest that time of day in the twilight, with his black suit, and he was a brave fucker he was, and was doing what he thought was right, raising the alarm, the bastard, and then we were lamming it over the grass trying to get out of that park and back into the city, but the cops were there in their big 4×4, Jaysus, and you can imagine the rest. And Jack got sixteen years for that because of his priors and I got ten because of mine being fewer than his but only just, and the judge said we were to serve every day of our sentences, and I certainly done that, which is to say, five years. For good behaviour. Yeh.

And another six months off for grassing up Jazzman Jack. Honour among thieves, I ask ya.

The filth kept that quiet. You know, in the interests of universal love. Not to mention me staying alive in the slammer.

'Young people of Ireland, I love you,' says your man John Paul.

That was very nice of him.

So, all things considered, it was going to take more than the ma crossing the river to Janet. It was going to take a miracle, says you. Oh, in fact, says you, it can't be done. Everything gone too far over, and that's that.

So that in some way – and I'm thinking on me feet here – lying down – I didn't really deserve no favour off Janet, but, since I'd got out of the Joy, I thought, I better – make an effort like. Jesus, I know I sound feeble.

Anyhows, here was me plan.

Oh, Jesus, when I think of it, it was a terrible plan.

But terrible plans for terrible situations, you know?

And it was all I could think of.

You know that ould feeling at school when the teacher asks ya a question, and you answer some pile of horseshit, and he looks at you, and he asks you what in the name of fuck do you mean, and you say, it was all I could think of? That was the nature of me plan.

Me plan, oh Jesus me plan. It sounded so good when I was in me cell in the Joy, and not a lot of things sounds good in there. As a matter of fact, it was the second plan I had. The first plan was more straightforward. The first plan was to go down to the '98 when I got out and kill the Afternoon Man, Dickie, even though he done me a lot of favours in the old days, and apart from being a murdering cunt wasn't such a bad fella.

But the Afternoon Man wasn't there, was he? Banged up with the other fucking loonies in Dundrum. The criminally insane, hah? They got that right. But howandever.

You know, a thing that always haunted me when Billy was killed was that we had to let him be buried on the parish, you know, up on the Angels' Acre in Glasnevin cemetery. I mean, we didn't have a shilling to put to a grave, no more than I will myself when I go. They can fucking throw me into the sea at Ringsend for all I care, and for all anyone might care. But a kid is a different thing, isn't it?

Yeh, it is.

You want, when you're so unlucky as to lose a kid, to have somewhere nice for him to lie, some nice plot of ground and a nice stone and bring the odd bunch of daffodils for him and all that the odd time, you know? You might say, well, the poor child is dead, and he won't know no differ, but, Jaysus it isn't for the dead that graveyards are made, it's for the livin' that does be left behind.

The dead maybe don't remember nothing.

I hope not!

Because when I'm dead I don't want to be thinking of everything still, unless I have one thought in me head as I lie, the thought of Janet. And I'd love when she's an old, old woman and dies herself, God rest her, for her to come in beside me wherever I might be put, but.

So, that was me plan, you see.

Hello.

Me plan was to go to Ringsend to the stonecutters there and get a little stone done out with Billy's name on it, and the date he died, and maybe put on it, 'Mourned by his Mam and Da', you know? The way they do.

The way normal people would, with money to do it.

Because I had the bit of money, I had the bit of money I took off the poor French boy, that I stuffed in me cacks before the cops nicked us.

Sacred money, it was, that I kept safe all the years of prison in me shoes. Like a fucking secret. I suppose that was an achievement in me life, as such, because, when you go into the slammer, the screws strip and shave you, and have a gawk down your throat, and a gander up your arse, and all the rest, but they never looked in me shoes. The flukiness of that. Some lads will tell you, you could smuggle an elephant into the Joy, but the screws are fairly vigilant. Mind you, if you get a bit of bad scag, you do be seeing elephants. But.

There musta been some Higher Power watching over that money.

To be honest now, at first I didn't know what I would do with it. You'd think maybe I would a' bought some gear with it, because the Joy is just a fucking junkies' paradise, there's more scag in the Joy than sugar.

But, I didn't.

I wouldn't let meself.

I mean, I bought scag alright, but not with that money. That money was fucking sacred.

The first thing of course I had to do before I could do the real first thing, was to do something about me habit. In Dublin, which I am told is now one of the richest cities in Europe, you don't just decide one day to get into a fucking programme and get yourself cleaned up. No, you have to fucking wait months and months to get into a fucking programme, so in the meantime you're still obliged to be on the ould heroin like, and do all the things you have to do to get it.

And then my name must a' come up on a list, and I went to Pearse Street like you do, with the other girls and boys, like it was school, and got hooked up for the methadone, you know.

As you start to come off the scag you can't believe what your former mates begin to look like. I mean, you start to see them as they are. Ghosts. Skinnied up and that dead man look in the face. And the funny thing is, you suddenly start to feel things, and one of the things you feel is a love for them, a sort a' desire to help them maybe, but you can't help them. That's funny, isn't it?

And, despite what people will tell ya, you really can get off the scag with the methadone, if you want.

You can.

It musta been in that time when I was obliged to be using that I got the virus off some cunt's needle.

And now here I am.

Light on Janet.

Janet So, I didn't hear from Joe for a good while after he got out. I knew he was out because people I knew and that knew him, seen him.

But of course I was living on the southside and he never roved out that way. I had heard long since he was using drugs so I was very glad not to be seeing him, and that he didn't try and see the boys. We were getting on just grand without him.

'Using drugs.' I just said it like it was a normal bit of news. Holy God. Joe. Full a' surprises. Joe Brady, that was afraid to take an aspirin when he had a cold. When the fucking District Nurse came to weigh Billy when he was a babby, and took a sample a' blood from his heel – or what did she do, stuck a needle into it for some fucking reason – Joe fainted. Not one of nature's junkies, Joe, he must a' worked at it. I don't know what that made me think when I heard it. I think it made me feel quite brutal, as in, good fucking riddance.

I was angry with him.

I had me memories of the good times with him and I often thought of them times, I still do, but I was definitely glad not to see him then.

You know.

Like all the times we used to go swimming at the Shelly Banks, when the kids were small, even before they were born. Joe and me and the kids, on the Ringsend bus.

You remember the old buses?

The conductor had a big leather bag like an elephant's scrotum, you know – isn't that a great word, I only learned that word off a doctor when little Macker had a swellin' there years ago – and he'd jingle his shillins and his pennies in it. 'Fares, please!' he'd shout, and there's none a' that now.

You'd think in the old days that things like that would be for ever.

And then you had to walk along the powerhouse wall, there was a lovely sandy road, and everyone from the city went out there in them days, and they wouldn't be seen dead there now, they're flying out to Marbella and all them places. But we didn't even know Marbella existed, and couldn't a' cared less, it was lovely on a sunny Dublin Sunday to reach the beach there along the Great South Wall, and lie down on our towels, and feel the lovely bake in the sun, and then crawl down to the water dead with the roasting, and fling yourself in, and the kids with the buckets, and maybe the poorer kids with wooden spoons out a' their mam's dresser, and the boys never had proper togs in them days, you should a' seen the gear they wore, maybe big ould knicks of their da's held on with a pin, but girls liked to have a nice one-piece, we called them, with a frilly bit under the breast, you know, ah yeh, like fucking Hollywood we thought we were.

Diving into that lovely water.

And the lovely sun.

And all.

And Joe saying, 'I'm only fucking roastin'.'

That sort a' thing.

I do remember that sort a' thing, you know.

And then I hear nothing and I'm probably not even thinking about Joe any more, it's that long a time, when this fucking letter comes. I have it in me pocket. Listen.

'Go to the Angel's Acre, please, Janet, do. Nine a' clock sharp Thursday morning coming.'

And a few other things, and how's everything and all that.

He never was no Shakespeare, my Joe.

No way was I going to go. He had wrote a few times before that, but I never paid no heed – whiney letters really.

Except it suddenly struck me, you know, that's where Billy's buried.

Maybe it's something about Billy.

And there wasn't another thing that could a' made me even think a' going, only Billy.

But I didn't want to go, because Joe bate the shite out a' me that night, and me wearing the green jersey and all.

And everything else, God knows. He said in court he never bate the young French lad, but somebody bate him. Bate him senseless. To death. His mother had to come from France to fetch him. Oh, Jesus.

But, but, but.

Yeh, I know. The fecking eejit.

It was Billy's love made me, and the love I had for Billy. Billy, my little boy, that was killed by a lorry in Parnell Street.

So I did, and I went to Glasnevin that day.

And I needn't a' worried, because there was no sign at all of Joe, he wasn't even there.

It was a very nice day that Thursday I remember, and someone was being buried as you might expect in a graveyard because there were a lot of big black cars at Kavanagh's pub.

It's all like years ago, that graveyard, Glasnevin is. You can't go in there without thinking what year it might be. Any ould year.

No year, maybe.

The Angels' Acre is just what it says, an acre of ground given over for the burying of angels. Childer that do be dead when they come out of the mothers, and poor people's childer that do die young.

A bit of ground with little crosses here and there, sometimes plastic flowers.

Holy ground, that's for sure.

And the people that lost the angels do come there, and yet still and all, it's always quiet there in my experience, and was quiet that day.

And I did weep when I saw it, of course, like I said I do weep sometimes.

Now a beautiful stone it was, just beautiful, with 'Billy Brady' wrote on it, and the day he was born and the day he died, just all perfect, in lovely letters. Good money paid for it, I'd say. And Joe had done that.

And the nicest thing was, he wasn't there.

He done it as a gift to me.

Not for himself, and getting back in with me. But for me. I thought that was very – admirable.

So I wrote him a letter. I got some blue-lined paper like I used to get off a' Patty in Lucky Duffy's when I lived down that way. I don't know if I mentioned Patty Duffy, but she's the nicest woman they ever put into a shop, let me tell you. When the bombs went off in '74, she was out helping all the dying souls, and her own head streaming with blood. I mean, I was only a chiseller at the time. I was only told she done that. But. So I got me the blue-lined paper and all, and I wrote me letter.

It was just a letter saying how happy I was Billy had his stone now, and I thanked him for the trouble he had took. And that I knew he knew it was special to me.

And then I said goodbye at the end, you know. Goodbye, sort a'.

Light on Joe.

Joe So – I got the beautiful stone made up and I went down to collect it when I heard it was ready.

I needed something to carry it so I found this ould wheelier in me ma's, and used that.

And I creep into Glasnevin with it, like it was a babby, you know, the stone.

And I was sort a' reminded of something, but blow me if I knew what it was.

(*Singing.*) 'The boys are back in town, the boys are back in town . . .' No.

That's life.

In the nice clear light of a Dublin morning.

Glasnevin is where all the heroes are buried, Michael fucking Collins and all. It's a lovely place really.

And I get to the Angels' Acre without a soul seeing me, and I hunted about for where we'd put Billy in, and it was very hard to tell where he was, it was that long since I visited, no sign of the wooden cross, but I thought maybe I knew where he was, and I dug a hole in the ground with a bit of an ould iron cross I found on a grave, and I put the stone in.

It was very heavy but it looked lovely.

And then this cunt of a guard arrests me.

I was seen pulling the cross off of an ould grave and someone called the pigs.

'What do you think you're doing?' he says.

'I'm not doing nothing,' I says.

'You're after defacing a memorial,' he says. I think that's what he said, but he had this thick culchie accent. 'And where did you get that buggy?'

'That what?' I said.

'The buggy.'

'Oh, the wheelier.' Sure, you'd need a translator for them culchie polis. 'I don't know, guard,' I says. 'But it was in me ma's, all legal like.'

'I'm taking you in,' he says, 'for vandalism. Have you ever been in trouble before?'

'Have I what?' says I. Does a bear shit in the woods? 'Listen,' I says, 'me wife is meeting me here in a minute, and I haven't even seen her for years, can you just turn a blind eye?'

And I told him the whole story. Just like I done to you, only leaving out bits, you know. I just gave him the gist.

His big culchie face listening.

He looked gobsmacked, his walkie-talkie crackling like a sort a' bird in his hand.

'I'm sorry,' says he, 'but I have to arrest you.'

'Can you not wait ten minutes behind a tree?' I says.

It was just a few minutes from nine o'clock. It was July and it was getting hot and the ould sparrows were flitting about. Chirping. I was sure Janet would come and I could show her what I done.

And then I thought, fuck it, how can I show her the stone and a fucking policeman waiting in the bushes for me? What are you thinking, Joe? She'd never fucking forgive me. Near Billy and all.

'Ah fuck it, guard,' I said. 'Sure you might as well take me in.'

That was the best decision I ever made in me life.

'Are you sure?' he says. 'Because I could wait if you wanted.'

Well, he didn't say that, of course. But, you know, he might have.

So off I go with my new friend, him with the ould wheelier under his arm.

And I got a bit of time in the Joy for my trouble.

Then I got a letter from Janet.

I thanked my lucky stars I hadn't been able to linger.

I did.

What a world.

Light on Janet.

Janet And then I didn't hear a blessed word from him, for a good while. I knew he was off the heroin though, because a friend told me.

Which was good.

I mean, I never wanted to see him again, but it's very hard to get off that drug.

I liked to think of him clean, you know.

That drug thing is so fucked up. So I was glad Joe got off it.

There was Joe the best part of seven year out of me life, but, you can't get completely away, you know – he's in your childers' faces. I'm looking at their faces, Jack as may be, and Joe's in there, like a face in a shop window,

47

kind a' floating. Oh Jesus, yeh. I wanted to put as much distance as I could between meself and Joe, but he was always there, in the faces of Jack and little Macker, wasn't he? Maybe I didn't always like that. I didn't like that he was always so close by, in his childers' faces. There were times, especially all them years he was in the Joy, and when me da was dead and everything seemed fucked up, I might a' shot Joe with a gun if I seen him in the street. But I couldn't a' seen him in the street. Because he was banged up a' course. Which was just as well.

Because he took everything away from me for a long time, and everything away from Jack and Macker, and everything away from himself.

Didn't he?

We didn't have much of a life maybe but it was a Dublin life, and every Dublin life is a life worth living, let me tell you. He might a' settled a bit, maybe scoped out a job somewhere. Everything in the country is getting that bit better. He might a' been working now. We'd be as old as we are and that's still young, in these days. We might a' been like those couples that have come through thick and thin, fighting the world. That's the secret. Fight the world, but not each other. You know? Fisticuffs, by all fucking means, but not against each other. That's the golden rule. If you break that, your future is gone. You're dead. It's all over.

After the letter I sent, saying goodbye, I upped sticks and moved meself and the boys out to Portrane. There was a job going there in the loony bin cleaning up after the loonies. Awful nice people some of them. Some of them are just animals, make you weep. People destroyed by something, I don't know. Gone back to nature. And the people looking after the loonies, some of them need their heads examined too. Shocking strange goings-on. It's like a madhouse sometimes. Well, yeh, it is a madhouse.

Portrane as you may know is by the sea, it's a seaside place, with a beach and all, which was lovely for Jack and Macker. Oh, they loved it there. And we had this fucking little tin hut in the grounds and they was down on the beach all times of the day, and went to fucking school in the village and everything. Oh, yes, oh, yes, happy days, and Joe should a' known what he was missing, what he lost, not that he would ever a' gone out so far from Dublin, he could only be happy breathing the air of Dublin, Joe's blood had Liffey water in it.

I felt it myself too. I used to lie in me doss on me own with the boys breathing in the little room next door, even in the long nights of August when it's daylight till eleven – isn't that the fucking nicest thing about Ireland? – I used to lie there and it was nice, yeh, it was lovely, but – it wasn't my Dublin, it wasn't Parnell Street, Cumberland Street and all the little dusty corners of things that I knew.

There was a fella there right enough, in the drugs department he was working, funnily enough, but, it never came to anything. It would a' been nice to get a bit of a ride off a' him, but, ah, I couldn't be bothered.

No, that isn't true.

To tell you the truth, I was a bit afraid of having anything to do with a fella. Because, marriage, you know, and going out with fellas – been there, done that, got the T-shirt. I mean, got the fucking T-shirt. Didn't I?

I'm like anyone else, I love a nice ride, I do, but, I don't know.

Stupid, since the ride was probably going free that time. A nice red-headed lad from Donabate he was.

Ah well.

Anyway, he was a bit on the neurotic side. You know? A man in need of rescue. But, fuck that.

Maybe it's not our job to be rescuing people. Maybe that's fucking God's job. Or your woman in the Phoenix Park. Or maybe there's only one or two people you have the strength to rescue, because it takes a huge fucking effort. Your kids maybe, your innocent kids, or your fucking husband.

Light on Joe.

Joe A bit of time must a' passed. Time flies when you're enjoying yourself.

My arse.

I tried to get going again at the robbing. It was hard, because I didn't have me contact, obviously.

And, I tell you, the bottom's fallen out a' that business. Too many at it. There's all sorts a' lads in Dublin now, very nice lads, Russians, Romanians. I think there must be a college for robbing in them countries, because these lads, they're professionals. It's a crying shame, a Dublin man can't hardly make a living at the robbing any more.

It's a terrible thing when a traditional trade goes to the dogs like that, yeh?

I'm only joshing.

It's just as fucking well.

Everything changes.

Anyway, I was feeling knackered a lot of the time.

I wasn't always well, you see. Up and down, like a hooer's knickers.

Me ma stuck by me till the day she died, heart failure, and I don't know, the day I stood by her graveside I felt very cold in me bones, like I could feel something creeping up, something dark and bad.

And I was hoping to see the boys there but they didn't come. And I don't blame them really.

Then, sad to say, I got really sick. Pneumonia first. Then pleurisy. Then TB. Then some sort a' cunting cancer. All off the ould virus, you know, courtesy of.

Which was sad.

But, you know.

I'm not looking for fucking sympathy.

No.

I don't even fucking deserve sympathy, and a run-over dog in the street deserves sympathy.

Because – I'm the man that bate up Janet Brady. Mrs Brady, the younger.

My wife.

The fucking pride a' Parnell Street.

Fuck it, and I did.

I said before I didn't, but that's fellas for you.

Fucking black liars, hah?

I'm sorry, I wasn't sort a' ready.

I'm ready now.

Yes, I hit her.

I smashed her lovely face in, I hit her till I heard bones breaking.

That was me, Joe Brady.

Macker to his ould ma.

Why did I fucking do that? I'll never know, only that I'm a mad bastard, and there must a' been evil in me afore I ever put the scag into me veins. All I ever fucking wanted was Janet and the kids, and maybe, yeh, okay, a job in the power plant where the river of hot water come out, and the little secret slabs a' soap in the wall for the men – ah, Jesus, pipe dreams. Fucking pipe dreams, Joe, me lad. You were never going to have a nice job like that and your fucking ma from North Summer Street and all the rest. There was nothing put the evil into meself only meself. And it wasn't Billy dying or nothing like that. And though this fucking virus is creeping up on me, creeping, what can I do about it? It's not like I don't care, I do care about it, I can't see how any living breathing person wouldn't. Because I want to fucking live. I want to see the bleeding new millennium that everyone's gassing on about. I want to fucking live.

Light on Janet and Joe.

Janet It's funny, when you're saying things, really trying to remember and tell the truth, there's another part of your head listening to it, and the other part of your head just now and then is saying, that's not true. I'm just noticing that now. Just sort a' noticing it. Because the part of you talking is the real part of ya, I mean, angry sometimes, and sometimes kinda weepy, and I suppose very hurt now and then, and oftentimes shy even.

Because, speakin' a' things not being true, that time Patty Duffy went out to comfort the dying in Parnell Street, that I was telling you about – yeh? I was a little girl then? Okay? Yeh, I was. But, I wasn't just told about it. I shouldn't a' said that, because it isn't true. And I only said it because I didn't want to be – going back.

I was a little girl in a little girl's set of knicks, you know, and some scaldy ould T-shirt I suppose if we had them then. You heard this huge bang. Everyone heard it. Even the boys and girls in the School for the Deaf heard it. I tell you.

I was about seven or eight. I went running out of me da's, and down the clattery iron steps. As I came up Cumberland Street I was walking slower and slower. I was looking, you see, big eyes out on stalks. I was on me own, I mean, I wasn't, there was loads of people milling about, crying, that was the first thing, tears everywhere I looked, tears and tears, and then me skinny legs bringing me to Parnell Street.

Oh my Jesus. The destruction. Who could tell you the proper tale of that? There was motor cars in weird places, you know, and every shop window was gone, blown out on the tarmac. At first I thought there was no noise, but it must a' been me ears or something, like I was swimming under the sea or something, because suddenly the noise came back on, screaming and such, and another sort a' noise, the fucking silence in the gaps between the noise, I don't know.

There was a parcel of something on the road in front of me. That's what I seen anyway. It looked like a parcel, with the wrappers blown off, meat or something, I thought it must a' been taken out a' a butcher's shop and dropped by someone, I mean, I was only a child that time, I didn't know. It was square, like the butcher cut it for someone, you know. But of course it wasn't out 'a a butcher's. No, no, it was a bit a someone.

Oh, my God. I never told this to no one before. I never. I'm shakin' to think about it.

Me skinny little legs for fuck's sake.

And Patty Duffy, the greatest woman that ever kept a shop, I tell you, the pride a' Parnell Street herself, a lovely big comfortable round woman, kneeling beside this poor man, like a fella in a war film with his legs blown completely off, oh he was, and Patty kneeling beside him, and whispering, yeh, yeh, and stroking his hand, like a mother. Oh, Patty Duffy, you were a saint that day.

They never even known who put them bombs there. Put them in cars and parked them and let them go off. So the bombs would kill the poor shoppers. It was about five o'clock I think it was. I think so.

You know, when you or anyone'd be shopping, and then heading home for the bus maybe, or if you were local, just heading home.

In Dublin. Heading home in Dublin. The place that I love.

There was a French lassie killed, I remember me mam telling me that. There was a couple killed just the like of Joe and me, with their two baby girls. Jesus. There was a baby killed not even born inside its mammy. Its mammy was its grave.

I call Patty Duffy the pride of Parnell Street because it was people like her put the pride back into the place after the desolation. In the months after, people could look back and remember how all the human feeling rose up in Patty and in themselves, and that they looked after the wounded and the dying and the dead, and cried for them, and stroked their suffering hands. There were gougers and layabouts there that day that came forward to help, that were made good by the occasion, as the priests would say – fucking redeemed they were.

Oh, Jesus, human pride.

Violence, you know.

Anyhow.

But, thinking about it, maybe that was why I was able to leave Joe. And not go back, I mean. Because when I was just a little girl I'd seen something so bad. You know? Evil. That you couldn't do nothing about. And then, hitting women, kicking your wife in the belly, where she made her babies, and punching her in the breast, that she fed them out of – you know – the same fucking thing. Only, you could do something about it. Feck off with yourself and the kids. Make a decent life.

Pride.

Jesus, I never meant to say all that, all the same.

Jesus, Jesus, I'm sorry.

Some things is private after all.

Where was I in me story? For fuck's sake. Oh yeh.

Lost me job in the loony bin, but, it's the new Ireland, isn't it?

God help us.

Jobs galore. Got a job in Geldof's factory, no bother. Yeh. Glad to see me. Uncle or something of your man that had us all sending money to Africa in the eighties, even I sent a few shillins, I did. A lovely singer, that wrote a lovely song about Monday. He never pushed on to Tuesday for some reason, I don't know why. He could a' covered the whole week, he was that good a singer, for God's sake.

Happy days. Happier, anyhow.

Little house from the council, southside, but only just, near the old gasworks on the docks, shades of me father, and Jack and little Macker teenagers, little no longer. Beautiful boys. Handsome, and it's not just me saying that. The very spit of Joe, both of them. Joe in his prime, in the old days, when I loved him.

And then I heard he was sick, the poor bollocks. I heard he was very very poorly as a matter of fact, that the poor bastard was down in the *Bon Secours* hospital, and I knew he probably didn't have many to go in and see him, and I also knew – oh, I also knew that he would be facing things bravely enough, because he is a brave man, all in all, except when he was being a coward that time, with me.

I knew that in the centre of everything, he was brave, like a soldier at the war. And that it was only life that done him in and made a fool of him, like it does us all.

Me fucking husband. You know.

She gets up slowly.

Joe (*singing*) 'Open up the Pearly Gates . . .'

Country Joe and the Fish.

Gear ould song.

Janet comes towards him gradually.

So I'm lying here on me hospital bed, when who comes in but Janet. She comes creeping in, I seen her, like a kid afraid of its da, like it done something wrong, but she never did do wrong, did she? And I'm lying there, feeling like shit, like maggots was in me brain, and no doubt, friends, looking like the plague, with rats in me skull and the long dreepy shite coming out me nostrils, a holy show if ever there was one.

Fucking hell.

Like the last fucking sinner in the deep part of hell maybe.

She comes in, creeping, in a nice way, drifting in, Janet, all the whole lot of her, looking a bit belted about by life and all, but, you know, herself. And I reckon when she gets to ninety that will still be Janet, just as nice as ever, just as fucking gear. And I'm feeling like shite as I say, but when I seen her, she was like a drug, straight into the old veins like, and such a fucking great ease sank into me, just to see her, because I hadn't even asked her to come, I was very content with the little letter. And she wasn't saying a word for the first few moments, only standing there looking at me, like she was trying to get in her head what to say.

Fucking hell.

Janet just by him now.

And then when I hear her voice, it's like ould music, the best of Thin Lizzy, or something as good as that.

'Howaya, Joe,' she says.

'Howaya,' I says.

'Fucking hell,' says she.

'That's just what I was thinking,' I says. 'But how and never, how are ya, seriously now?'

'I never been better till I seen you, Joe. Jesus, Joe, what ha ya done to yourself?'

'I don't even fucking know,' I says. 'I done meself in, I fucked meself up. I suppose that's what I done. How are them boys?'

'The boys are grand, Joe.'

'The boys are good?' I says.

'Oh, yeh,' she says. 'They're grand, they're only doing great.'

'They're not mitchin' off a' school or anything?'

'No, they're not, they're good boys. Big boys.'

'Ah, yeh, sure I knew that, big boys,' I says.

'Ah, yeh,' she says, 'sure Jack's going out working next year.'

'He should try the power station.'

'What?' she says.

'Try for a job there. You know, in the station, shovelling the coal, and cleaning off after in the ould river of hot water.'

'Oh, Janey,' she says, 'with the soap in the walls.'

'Yeh,' I says.

'Heh, heh, heh,' she says, you know, laughing. 'Well, no, he wants to go on the buildins.'

'To fucking England?' I says.

'No, Joe. Dublin. The Financial Services Centre. The docklands and all.'

'The what?' I says.

'The docklands,' she says.

'Oh,' says I. 'Like your da before him.'

'Yeh,' she says, 'like the da, only not working the ships. Buildin' the new offices and all.'

It was then I knew she still loved me. Not straight away knew it.

But it was something about me saying about the power station and her mentioning the soap, and the little laugh. Yeh, yeh, it was the little laugh that gave her away.

And the pride welled up in me. Pure pride. Like sugar it was.

'Well,' says I, not letting on, and I never would let on, 'I haven't long for this world anyhow, Janet,' I says. 'No loss, says you.'

We were swimming then, in the sunshine, it was like we were swimming in the cold water of Dublin Bay, just her and me, when we were young, at the Shelly Banks, and everything washed away.

'Well, everyone is a loss to the world when they die,' she says.

'That's right, I suppose,' I says. 'That's right,' I says.

She touches his hand. Her wedding ring must be visible to him. He doesn't dare move.

The happiest man in Dublin – (*Closes his eyes.*) The happiest.

Janet (*looking out*) Ya see?

They're in the light there a few moments together, and then no light.